The Truth Is
The Hardest Pill
To Swallow

Shannon Branch

This book is a brutally honest, truthful, and accurate guide to life, love, relationships, marriages, dating, and sex from the perspective of a single black male who has experienced a lot as well as witnessed much from life. NO sugar coating, NO fairy tales, NO feminist or sexist nonsense. Just telling it how it is. The way it SHOULD be told. Now let's get to it.

CONTENTS

FELLAS

OUTRO

SHANNON BRANCH

INTRO

1. WHAT DEFINES "TRUTH"?

TRUTH :

noun \ ' *trüth* \ :
the state of being the case: the body of real things, events, and facts: actuality, often capitalized: a transcendent fundamental or spiritual reality

The truth is what exists, what can be proven, explained, based off of experiences as well as observations. A lot of people confuse truth with opinions. As well as misuse the phrase "that's your opinion", every time someone says something that may be deemed as outrageous, or difficult to understand. The word "opinion" is usually tossed around by stubborn people who can't see past the typical norm. Truth is based on the obvious, things we can physically see, touch, prove, and explain--based off true facts from what we notice, as well as what we can back up. A lot of what we speak is opinions, ideologies based off what we feel as opposed to what we see.

This book you just purchased contains nothing but TRUTH: real life events, spoken from the perspective of an observer. These are NOT "opinions", because everything I state in this book can be physically PROVEN. It's difficult to accept anything outside the box, or to accept what may be unusual, or rare, but the truth is disturbing. We often ignore the obvious because we rather focus on the possibility, and keeping faith in things or people we want can often prevent us from using something that we all have, but rarely use: COMMON SENSE. So this book is a breakdown of relationships, dating, sex, from a common sense angle. Telling it how it is, no sugar coating, no feminism, or any sexist nonsense. Just pure uncut, raw TRUTH.

This book will be VERY controversial. It will attack a LOT of stereotypes and standards in society dealing with the opposite sexes. It will help couples, marriages, and single people as well. It will help many recognize their worth, as well as recognize GAME. This book will give you the do's, the don'ts, the pros, the cons, and tips for relationships, marriage, dating, and sex. This book will be the end all be all of relationships, dating & sex 101, and will provide a much needed sense of pure honesty, realism, and common sense. This book will assist you in making decisions that are difficult to make-- whether you should stay or go. I will reveal a lot of secrets to females that guys don't want females to know as well as the secrets that females don't want us guys to know. The sole purpose of this book is to make you think, re-evaluate, as well as gain motivation, self-worth, and understanding. A lot of people may disagree, or oppose what is contained in this manual, but like the title says :

THE TRUTH IS THE HARDEST PILL TO SWALLOW.

So please read with an open mind, and also understand that the truth is ALWAYS in **BLACK** & *WHITE*...

So let's begin shall we?

2. WHY MOST RELATIONSHIPS TODAY FAIL

If you take time to notice your surroundings, you will see a lot of people falling for the same trap. The same games. The same lies. Ever wondered why? We all want that special someone to call our own, and we usually second guess our own pre-judgment and ignore red flags to obtain it. It's without some form of betrayal in the process. Relationships today are almost impossible to maintain without one or the other trying to scheme. The best part of being romantically involved with someone is the emotional and physical fulfillment, but what about the mental? Your mind is usually taken through a constant roller coaster of mixed signals, disturbing vibes, and numerous doubts. The question is, why do relationships mainly fail? Why do most marriages end in divorce? This is why you should keep reading, especially if you want to learn how to make your current or next relationship last forever. I'm here to teach you...

In this piece we'll touch on the issues of why relationships today fail, and then we will focus on the solutions of what it takes to make a relationship last a lifetime. Now you're probably thinking to yourself "what does this guy know?" right? Well obviously you trust my insight to some extent if you're reading this. Never underestimate a person's level of knowledge dealing with relationships. You never know what that person been through. Or what you can learn from that person. I been through a LOT dealing with women, as well as being VERY observant of my surroundings, and I take notes from successful marriages, as well as unsuccessful marriages, and apply those do's and don'ts to my own personal situations. We can all learn from each other, as well as teach each other. So allow me to guide, educate, and teach you to the best of my ability based off what I seen and experienced personally, and externally. Now let's get into it shall we?

The #1 reason why most relationships today fail is due to lack of communication. You would think by technology rapidly advancing and making communicating much easier than it was when our grandparents and elders were coming up (my grandmother has a Facebook and Twitter. scary) that more people would know how to communicate right? WRONG. Technology has made communication amongst each other WORSE. Text messaging has eradicated the simple concept of picking up a phone and holding a real conversation. People rather type back and forth instead of hearing each other's voice. This is a problem. It causes trust issues within a relationship when a couple sends texts and gets late replies. Or NO reply at all. Instead of thinking the best case scenario (he/she could be sleeping, or the phone could be charging, etc.) it's usually the worst case scenario being thought about (he/she could be cheating, or he/she is ignoring my calls/texts, etc.) so cell phones basically cause problems in relationships, and destroys trust. Dramatically. So many people get so used to texting a conversation by using simple one liners and smiley face icons, they have nothing to say to each other in person. Sad.

Another huge factor in why most relationships fail today is the internet. Mark Zuckerberg sat in his college dorm room and blindly created a website that he had no idea would control almost every man and woman's relationship in the world today. Facebook is a serious issue. Married men get caught up all the time by flirting on Facebook, writing on another woman's wall, inboxing women, and leaving inappropriate content on his page. Women too. Many women who have boyfriends will claim to be "single" on Facebook, or will act is if they are single by constantly uploading vulgar pics of herself posing half-naked in the bathroom, or by "liking" a bunch of random guys photos.

Some women even engage in cheating through instant chat conversations on Facebook as well as on sites like Skype, that are virtually undetectable by their boyfriends, unless he is standing right over her shoulder the entire time. The internet has ruined thousands, if not millions, of relationships. We can't blame Mr. Zuckerberg for this, or any founder of a social site or dating site, but we can blame the level of temptation that a social site like Facebook, MySpace, or even Twitter causes. It makes flirting and cheating almost impossible to spot. Social sites also disconnects actual real life communication from each other, and sometimes, even the world.

We spend so much time speaking behind a computer and cell phone, we forget how to speak in real life. They say communication is 90% non-verbal. Communication is mainly body language, eye contact. So it isn't just by talking over the phone, it's also by communicating face to face. Especially when there's an issue. That goes into my next targeted point of why most relationships fail: selfishness. Selfishness causes a person to shut down, not express their feelings or views in attempt to avoid an argument, which never works because not fixing a problem only creates more problems. Being stubborn, and lack of effort are recipes for disaster. This is one of the biggest downfalls in ANY relationship, whether its business or personal. You can't just consider your own views and feelings, in a relationship it's not just about YOU. It's about each other. A relationship is supposed to be a team effort. Not a one man army.

So many of us have this "give little and receive all" mentality in relationships, and it don't work that way. This is why I dumped my last girlfriend. She was VERY selfish and self-centered. Everything had to be about her. She didn't understand how to reciprocate what she demanded. Or the concept of earning a man's trust and effort. She was used to every guy kissing her ass and letting her walk over them, she couldn't handle a man who wasn't a pushover, or naive. So she lost out on a great man who was loyal and real with her. Just like many other women who feel like they deserve the world without bringing any effort to the table. What causes this? It starts with the upbringing.

The mother or father usually brainwash the girl into thinking she's a "princess", and she is entitled to a man's 100% without matching it. It's also due to her surroundings, such as her girlfriends, who are always putting some negative garbage in her ear about guys. Or her mother is bitter based off her own failed relationships or a failed marriage, so she teaches her daughter how to hate men, and use men. As far as why guys are selfish? The same factors. Listening to their favorite rappers and singers degrade and use women, making them think it's cool to be a "player". Or listening to their home boys, who also have no clue on how to appreciate a woman. It's very rare that you see an influential person in the world educating our youth on how to treat each other, and how to value a good man/good woman. It's frustrating.

So what are the solutions to making a relationship last forever? It's actually very simple. The first step is accepting your partner for who he/she is, and not trying to change or mold that person into what YOU want him/her to be. The next step is learning how to communicate with each other as well as treating each other with respect. By talking to each other, and not at each other. It's okay to argue, but it's not okay to bicker and yell at each other and talk over each other. A lot of us let our egos ruin our relationship. In a relationship there should be NO ego. That only works when your single, and if you bring your ego into a committed relationship, then you will remain single for a very long time. You have to put forth the same amount of effort you put in during the beginning. Meaning you have to be consistent and reliable.

Always remember what made you fall in love with that person, and focus on just that. Not the flaws. Nobody is perfect. Including YOU. Don't expect someone to put forth more effort than you either. A relationship is about 50/50 effort. You get out what you put in. No double standards. And lastly, you have to trust your partner, if you can't trust your partner, then that's not the right person for you. If you always have a "gut feeling" about your partner, then it's probably true, and you should get out of that relationship. Your "gut feeling" rarely lies to you. There's a huge difference between being paranoid, and having strong senses and a keen instinct to detect something that isn't right. My grandmother who raised me taught me as a child to always follow my "gut feeling", because it's usually God telling me the truth about a person or situation. My grandmother never lied to me. Ever.

The truth is there's millions of reasons why a relationship can fail. I just chose to speak on a few major ones that most of us can relate to. Some of us experienced things that some of us haven't. The main thing is learning from those experiences and not bringing that baggage into the next relationship. So if you want a successful relationship, I encourage you to treat your partner how you want to be treated. Don't just take, but give also. Be supportive of each other. Stop focusing on the "roles of the gender" and start focusing on what makes each other happy. If your partner likes flowers, then buy them flowers every now and then. Just don't overdo anything. Try to avoid petty arguments. Learn how to let things go. Going back and forth over everything can cause your partner to regret being with you. If your partner tells you how he/she feels, listen. Don't be so quick to get defensive. Relationships are about compromise and sacrifice. Team effort. No selfishness. Ever. Or it won't work. Always remember: it's not all about YOU. It's about EACH OTHER.

LADIES

3. A MESSAGE TO THE LADIES

LADIES: NEVER let a man, or a "n**ga" break you. Walk over you. Use you. Mistreat you. EVER. You are a QUEEN. You come from GOD...not a sewer. GOD created you to be a POWERFUL FORCE in this world, by using your MIND, STRENGTH, and WISDOM...but society brainwashed females into using their BODIES instead. There's nothing wrong with "looking sexy" and "getting attention", but when it ONLY brings you disrespect, then it's NOT worth it ladies.

I want you to understand that I'm ONLY saying this because I DON'T like seeing women playing themselves, or with low self-esteem, NOR do I want to see ANY woman get hurt, or lied to, or screwed over. I've watched my own mother get mistreated by men, as well as many women in this world. That's why I talk about the things I do, because I CARE. Not too many of my so called "brothas" can say the same, because most of my "brothas" too busy trying to be "playas" and following these dumb ass rappers who are mostly ignorant and uneducated themselves. I'm trying to make the concept of treating real women right COOL again. Because when you take good women, real women for granted, you get NOTHING in return for it, but a big ol' dose of that KARMA.

So I want Each and Every One of you LADIES to stop taking SH*T off these "N**GAS" and recognize YOUR WORTH!

You are too BEAUTIFUL to allow yourself to be treated so UGLY!!!

Always remember: you are a QUEEN. NEVER LET ANYONE TELL YOU DIFFERENT!

QUESTION :

What would WONDER WOMAN do in a situation if she's mistreated or taken for granted by a man?

ANSWER :

That would NEVER happen, for 3 reasons...

1.) WONDER WOMAN is a GODDESS.
2.) She knows her worth.
3.) SHE WILL KICK HIS ASS!!!!!!

So ladies, next time a guy gets out of line, ask yourself: How would WONDER WOMAN handle this?

4. WHAT DEFINES A TYPICAL FEMALE?

Typical females never display any original identity. She talks, dresses, walks, thinks, and acts like every other female, and swears up and down how she's "nothing like other females out here".

She usually has kids with different men and be still "looking for friends"...instead of a HUSBAND. She lives her life as if she DONT have kids. Still clubbing, still bopping every weekend.

She actually thinks "looking for friends" is realistic. She doesn't overstands that you can't LOOK for friends. And she loves to throw the word "friend" around to describe anyone she knows personally.

A typical female mistakes "male friends" for OPTIONS. She has a team of guys she keeps around to boost her ego and self-esteem. This type of female is a COMPLETE waste of time for any man who is looking for wife material.

She loves to lead guys on to nowhere. The type to give a guy her number just to ignore his calls when he calls her and say he a "stalker".

She loves to argue even when she know she is wrong. She never takes accountability for anything she does. She blames everything she does wrong on men and use excuses to justify everything she does.

She has over 1000 friends on Facebook...and 95% of them are random dudes she never speaks to.

She takes hundreds of pictures of herself...in the bathroom...half naked...with a camera phone. And swears up and down she's a model.

She logs on to Social Media everyday but swear up and down how she "don't be on Social Media like that".

Typical females love attention. No matter what kind it is as long as guys notice her she feels empowered. She dresses like a slut and gets offended when she's approached like one.

Typical females are very naive and dumb. They base "good men" off of material assets and superficial attributes.

She demands respect but has no clue on how to EARN respect.

Her idea of "having fun" is going to the club, and going to the bar. That's it. She has no taste in cultured things at all. She only does things that gains her attention.

She love to say how she "don't need no man to do nothing" for her but she wants a man who has money, a car, his own place, a "good job", etc.

Her ideal type of man is "tall, handsome, respectful, intelligent, blah blah blah...but NEVER chooses that. Instead she chooses the guys who has multiple baby mamas, felonies, no education, no job, etc.

A typical female loves to broadcast her relationship on Facebook as if Facebook is her best friend. She fails to realize that no one really cares...except for the other typical females she socializes with who also have no life.

She spends her entire day on Social Media. She is detached from the REAL world.

She believes a man should "wait" to have sex with her so he can "get to know" her first.

She claims she "don't hang with females" because they all phony, or they all like to keep up drama, or

some other bogus reason on why she likes to be around a bunch of dudes instead.

Typical females love to talk about other females negatively. She quick to put another sista down for doing the same thing SHE does. Only difference is the typical female tries to hide her dirt.

Typical females love running game. They are very inconsistent too. Meaning if you're a guy and you meet her and you hold a conversation with her on the phone on Monday, you won't get a call or answer from her until Wednesday at the closest...or sometime the next week. Her excuse? "I'm a busy person".

Unreliable? Definitely. You make plans with this type of chick and you better have a strong plan B. A typical female rarely does anything she says she's going to do.

She believes since she's a "woman" the man is supposed to take her out on the first date.

She wears makeup, hair weave, fake nails, fake eye contacts with bogus colors (dark skinned women do NOT have blue eyes), but she quick to call herself a "real woman".

THE TRUTH IS THE HARDEST PILL TO SWALLOW

She's married still on Social Media adding random dudes. WHAT IS THE PURPOSE?

She adds random dudes on Facebook for no reason and use the line "its networking" as an excuse.

She claims to be a "Christian" but LOVES horror movies.

She believes that a male and a female can have sex and be like brother and sister afterwards.

She believes a guy who approaches her can be like her brother with no intentions on having sex with her or being intimate with her.

Typical females are quick to get defensive when you tell them the truth about themselves. They can't handle criticism. They so brainwashed that when you tell her the TRUTH about herself she rejects it.

She likes to show off her body but wonder why no guy takes her serious.

She has no personality at all. On the phone she just sits and hold the phone. Never has anything to say, but as SOON as you say something she don't like she QUICK to talk then...and will cut you off while you're talking in the process.

She never listens. She only waits for her turn to talk. She can care less what you have to say. She going to do what she wants to do regardless because she a "grown ass woman".

Her favorite word is "independent" but in reality she is VERY dependent on men. Her whole existence is based off of what a MAN told her she was and is.

A typical female is probably YOU...or someone you know of...or someone your currently involved with. Either way, typical females are the WORST. They will generate nothing but problems and headaches for you ultimately resulting in a complete waste of your time.

Typical females come in various shapes, sizes, and colors, but the SAME mentality. Stay away from these losers. They may look and portray to be "real women" but these chameleons will get you nowhere in life. So fellas make sure your woman has NONE of these traits or you can forget about that thing called marriage. And ladies make sure YOU don't have any of these traits, or your just going to be "jump off" material for a very long time.

5. THE DIFFERENCE BETWEEN WIFE AND "WIFEY"

A young lady on twitter asked me what's the difference between being a wife and being a "wifey". I started to laugh but I had to realize that many women today honestly don't know what separates the two, let alone the true definition of being a wife anymore. Most sistas just want to get married, but not many actually want to be a wife. I see so many women bragging about how she's some guys "wifey" which in my opinion is a low standard for any woman. So I will compare and contrast the difference between wife and "wifey.

A WIFE...

Never has to compete with other women because she is the only woman her man is seeing, "talking to", and interested in. She knows this from his actions. Not just his words.

The wife knows her man's family and friends. She usually has her man's parents or guardians blessings. Along with his friends. If her lifelong partner's friends and family don't approve of her chances are she isn't going to be his wife.

A man treats his wife with the utmost respect. Never cheats on her, or lies to her, or treat her like a jump-off, a "main" or his "wifey".

The wife usually sees a side of her partner that no one else sees. She knows her man inside and out. His darkest thoughts, secrets, etc. There are no mysteries. No cloudy areas. Everything is in the open.

The wife is the woman who a man chooses to spend the rest of his life with. She gets the marriage proposal, the ring, and everything that man has to offer her for a lifetime.

A "WIFEY"...

Is the woman who a man spends all of his time with. Usually been with for a long time. Maybe even live with. But isn't married or engaged. Ever thought why? Keep reading...

Men know whether he is going to marry a woman in the early stages of the relationship. It takes us men no time to see if a woman is going to be around for a while...or a lifetime.

The "wifey" also has met SOME of his family, and SOME of his friends. Sometimes the "wifey" may

receive the man's family and friends blessings, but it's usually over ruled by him...in the end.

The "wifey" is equivalent to the "main". Meaning the one who he likes or cares about the most out of the women he deals with. The "wifey" is rarely the only one. Just in HER mind she is. But she don't know the TRUTH. Men are NEVER 100% faithful to a "wifey". Here's why...

The "wifey" is the woman who he may spend years with. In his heart he knows he won't marry her though. He'll keep her around until the woman who he feels in his heart he WILL marry comes into his vision, then its curtains for the "wifey". A man is going to be faithful or dedicated to the "wifey" for so long before he starts roaming. He will eventually break up with the "wifey" and go be with the woman who he will make his WIFE.

So ladies...please stop bragging about how your his "wifey", all that means is your his TEMPORARY wife until the PERMANENT wife comes along. Then it's back to the drawing board for you. Don't be stupid. If you don't have a ring on your finger then you're just his girlfriend. "Wifey" is a very low standard to claim.

6. WHY DO MEN DEGRADE WOMEN?

The reason why so many men treat so many women like objects is simple: It's because A, the vulgar, disrespectful, ignorant approach that he takes with the woman he approaches obviously has been effective for him in the past. B, he feels for some reason that he has every right to approach the woman like a whore on the strip. C, he doesn't even know how to approach a woman, so instead of being respectful and polite, he uses lines that he heard one of his homeboys or one of his favorite rappers say. Or finally D, he has a lack of confidence in himself, so he chooses to attempt to bring the female that he approaches confidence down along with his in order to get what he wants. Either way that he chooses, it's all unacceptable.

Now, as a man I can honestly say that I have been very disrespectful towards females at times. But in my defense, it was aimed at the type of females who deserved it, because they don't even respect themselves. And you can't save a hoe. Those type of females don't even get put in the same category as women. If a man even thinks of approaching a "bop" like a lady, he will get NOWHERE. Trust me, I know.

Some females leave us men no choice but to be brutal and raw with them. If we're not, then we'll be labeled as "soft". I've experimented different approaches with women only to see the naked truth. Women are not used to a man being respectful towards her, so when a man IS actually very respectful towards her, SHE is disrespectful towards the man! She may feel like he's running some tired game(which most men are), or she may not feel like being bothered. Now with that said, we all know that a man's pride, confidence, and ego is worn on his sleeve right? So what do you think is the average reaction from a man after rejection? "Aww f*ck you b*tch!", "b*tch you ain't cute!", or "I just wanted to f*ck anyway!" and a bunch of other blah blah right? Now pay attention...

The bottom line is, you can't even tell the difference from a lady, a hoe, a b*tch, or a bop to the physical eye! So the average man is only used to meeting the females who ARE bops, hoes, and b*tches, but NOT ladies. So out of routine, men tend to use the SAME approach to get with that particular female, because he's only used to meeting females who have no polish. It makes sense. Now, for the ladies reading this, you must understand that every female feels she is a lady, so don't be upset when you get approached like a slut from some stank breath, cheap cologne, bling-blong rocking ass clown who come at you with the "ay shawty..." approach. Just shake your head and keep it moving, because believe it or not ladies, THAT approach really works with SOME females. It's pretty pathetic.

So, if you're tired of getting treated like sh*t ladies, this is what you do: Stay away from the bops in your click that you call your "friend", trust me, she will only bring YOUR stock down. And men judge women based off who they hang around. Also, stop dressing like the type of female you hate being called. Your dress code, and body language tells us everything about you. And finally, stop expecting men to KNOW what type of female you are. You as a lady have your own personal responsibility to carry yourself like the woman you are, so if a man comes at you wrong, then treat him like the child that he is. Don't feed into it. Only bops explain themselves. a woman doesn't need to.

To all the fellas reading this, treat females the way they deserve to be treated. Hoes, bops, and b*tches get no respect. But if you do happen to meet a woman, then honor her like you would want a man to honor your mother, grandmother, sister, aunt, or cousin.

7. WHY DO WOMEN DEGRADE THEMSELVES?

My biggest concern with women has always been how they present themselves to the public eye. it makes no sense to me how a woman can be so beautiful on the outside, but be so hideous on the inside. Us men continue to treat our women how they basically treat themselves. I look at how many females actually come to the club with inappropriate clothing on. Way too many. It's pretty disturbing that women will do any f*cking thing to get attention. Even if it costs them their self-respect.

If you turn on your tel-lie-vision what do you see y'all? Big booty "hoes" all oiled down with big bouncy tits in the video gyrating next to your favorite rapper on BET, MTV, and VH1. You could even go on Facebook, and you'll find plenty of our women looking like out of shape porn stars who need some serious one-on-one time with the treadmill. Why do y'all continue to dress like sluts ladies? But get upset when men call y'all "hoes" and "b*tches"? I have two little sisters who both get on Facebook, and I teach them the concepts of self-respect. But women who do have common sense unlike a little girl, should be a better example for our young ladies growing into grown women. Instead of looking, even acting like a 9th grader, women should carry themselves with the self-respect that they all demand from us men so much.

It all starts with self-esteem. A lot of our women lack confidence in themselves, so they go out to get assurance. A lot of our ladies feel that they're only attractive when dressed up. It's sad. Women who go to the corner store for a pack of cigarettes should not be wearing f*cking stilettos!!!! A woman who goes to a PTA meeting at her child's school should not be looking like Beyoncé on the "Upgrade U" video!!!! Women have really dug themselves in the hole by continuing to degrade their own mind, body, and aura for attention and financial gain. It's time to wake up ladies. Stop getting upset when you get called a "bop" when you know that what you are. If you feel that your such a "lady", then why does every man call you different? Think about it.

A man senses a woman who respects herself, and he has no choice but to respect her if he plans on getting with her. Us men do not fall for the games that most women play, we just play along. For example, I met a very attractive young lady who tried to convince me she's still a virgin right? But that very night she's giving me, and my three homeboys the best head of our life!!! Sh*t like this is why men don't listen to anything that comes out of a woman's mouth. Anybody can talk a good game. But only fools fall for it. Men aren't concerned with image and reputation, so we don't have to portray an image to get what we want. Sadly, a lot of us do, but it's not needed. Same thing for a woman, you don't have to put on a front to get what you really want. Just be who you are. If you like being a "bop", then cool. Just don't get mad when men call you one, if you like dressing like a slut, that's cool too. Just deal with the approach that you're bound to get from people around you by carrying yourself in whatever manner YOU choose.

If you are a woman who don't dress like a slut when you go out, I commend you. If you are a woman who understands that men are NOT trying to be your "friend"...unless he is gay...I also commend you. And to all the beautiful ladies who feel y'all have to be half- naked in order to be noticed, I pray for y'all. The truth is, every woman loves attention, but it's how you go about getting it. Keep your f*cking clothes on ladies!!!!

If you have to sell yourself in order to achieve the material things that makes your pussy wet, then you need to re-evaluate life and YOURSELF. A man who spends money on you probably don't respect you. If a man goes out of his way to give you things out of pure kindness and benevolence, fine. But to the females who try to manipulate men into buying you things in order to have sex, you just put a price tag on yourself. And that alone makes you a f*cking scumbag. A real woman understands that respect is earned, not given.

IF I have offended you in any way, then I apologize for being TRUTHFUL..

8. GUYS WITH LOW STANDARDS

I'm sure you have a friend that's a guy and he's always talking about "where the hoes at?" Yeah...that guy. Or the so-called "playa" that's always bragging about how many "bad b*tches" he got...but you NEVER see NONE of his so-called "bad b*tches". Or what about the dude who has a faithful, beautiful woman, but yet he has a "side-chick". Or how about the homeboy that's always thirsty for some ass talking about "c'mon son hook me up with one of your friends I don't even care how she look". Have you ever took time and asked these type of thirst buckets what their standards are when it comes to women?

Probably not. Probably because you could care less, but if you took time to ask these cats what type of women they deal with, the response you usually get is STAGGERING. A LOT of these dudes out here have NO standards.

They will have sex with ANYTHING. I know guys who will smash ANY female that's willing to give it up, without thinking twice. She can be HIDEOUS, sloppy as f*ck, stankin', musty, dirty ass feets, filthy house, and he will STILL smash on the low. I mean where do these type of n*ggas come from???

How do you detect if he has low standards, or NO standards at all??? Let's talk about this...because dudes with low standards are the #1 reason why soooooo many raggedy ass females be walking around thinking they dimes trying to act exclusive.

THIS MUST STOP. NOW. I mean let's be honest, EVERY guy has smashed at least ONE female he would NEVER take in public. But making it a constant thing? That's having low standards. We ALL as men had our "thirsty for some dome/clap moment" and we hopped in the first chicks' mouth that was willing to suck as well as the first chicks' vagina that was willing to spread. But making that a routine is NOT a good look. I personally don't even associate with dudes like this. Mainly because it makes me look bad as if I have no standards either. You can't even take these type of clowns with you anywhere because they're embarrassing!

You go to the mall with a homeboy and he running up to every female that walks past him, or y'all go to a bar together to shoot some pool, and he talking about "look at them hoes over there"...and one of em' got hairy feets, a MEAN overbite, and her belly is overlapping her jeans. SMH You have stay away from these type of dudes. They pose a threat to a relationship also...meaning if you leave your girl around him, there's a HUGE possibility he might try to make a move on her. Why? Because that's what thirsty dudes do!

Now you wonder WHY guys who constantly lie, scheme, cheat, and sleep around continue to do it with females of low quality. Well it's pretty simple. Guys usually choose females they feel are equal to them. So if he cheats on a good woman for a low life chick, then he subconsciously sees himself as a low life guy. If he makes poor decisions with women, such as having unprotected sex with females he barely knows (which causes most baby daddy/baby mama situations) then he wasn't raised properly or taught how to value and appreciate a woman. So a lot of a man's ways come from his upbringing as well as his surroundings.

I recommend each one of you to carefully observe the company you keep, because the saying of "birds of the same feather flock together" is VERY true. If you have standards, then hanging around dudes with NO standards will only hurt you in the end.

So fellas: keep dudes around you that keep bad females around them...and ladies: understand that it's not always your fault if a guy decides to sleep with another woman. You just dealing with a guy with low standards. Real men don't cheat or take a good woman for granted. So if you do everything you supposed to do, and he still messes around with another chick who is 95% less attractive,

JUST REMEMBER WHAT I TOLD YOU.

9. 10 WAYS TO KEEP YOUR MAN

You ever wondered WHY so many men cheat? Well ladies it's quite simple...too many women lack the ability to keep their man happy. Many of today's women excel at getting a man to want them, but they have no clue on how to keep him. Pleasing us men isn't hard to do at all, so why do you think women have such a hard time then? If you look around, many women make everything about themselves, instead of about each other. That's one main reason why men cheat or leave. Amongst many others...but that's another topic. But for the ladies who want to know what us men REALLY want, keep reading. Here I will break down 10 ways to KEEP your man happy, and faithful.

1. Sex on the Regular: Pretty Self-Explanatory ladies. .Initiating sex shows that you are still sexually attracted to him. If he doesn't get it from you then even the most committed men will get it from someone else.

2. Cook a couple of times a week: A good home cooked meal by his woman will always keep him in line. A man will never cross a woman who cooks for him. It goes back to when he had his mother cooking for him.

3. He will want nothing but yours. True story.

4. Prove to him that he is the only ONE, Not the important one: This does not apply to those with open relationships...and what type of woman has those anyways?...but if you ARE the one who wants him to be faithful to you, it goes both ways. Telling him he is the only one is not enough. He has to know it in his heart. You MUST really show him that he is the only person you are interested in. If he feels that he is one of a few, it doesn't matter if he is the "main", he will start to build a team of his own.

5. Have Discussions not Arguments: When faced with problems and differences have a discussion that includes both people speaking about the issue and both people listening. Don't yell, cut-off, or over talk him. Same goes for him. Men hate a nagging woman. The more you do this the more he will search for someone who doesn't do that. And there are women who know how to have discussions without arguing. So make sure YOU are one of them.

6. Take him out on a date once in a while: There are a couple of reasons that this is effective. One, it shows that you care enough for him to spend what you have on him. Two, it shows independence not dependence. It shows that you have your sh*t together and you don't depend on a man to feed your ass. It's not like you have to make a habit out of it but it makes a nice surprise and keeps things interesting in your relationship.

7. Don't Change Him: Allow progressive growth. Trying to change a man from who he is shows he is really not your ideal guy. It shows no confidence in his character and you are with him simply to mold him. In return it drives him away from the personality that you are putting out.

8. Being Honest: Even when it will hurt you or him, you have to be honest in every situation. Telling him something that you know he will not want to hear will hurt at first, but it will also build trust in you. The more you do this the more he'll respect you.

8. Be productive: Nothing is worse than a woman who sits on Facebook or Twitter all day with no purpose, or who constantly has to 'kick it" and "go out". Step your game up Hun, a man only respects a woman who handles her business and has goals and hobbies ("going out" isn't a hobby ladies). If you expect your man to have a job, car, own place, etc. you must be able to possess the same.

9. Know how to listen, not just talk: This is the most important form of communicating: listening. Not just hearing what YOU want to hear. So when your man has something to say, hear him out. Even if he talks in novels, just hang in there. You'll be surprised by how much you learn from your man by listening...hopefully yours has something meaningful to say, and if he don't...then why is he your man?

10. Have something to relate about: A relationship isn't possible without a bond, or "friendship". Physical attraction, sex, financial stability, status, etc. is NOT going to hold up your relationship sista. You have to have at least ONE thing you and him can both relate about. Or you going to be in for a rude awakening.

10 WHAT DEFINES A GOOD MAN?

A GOOD MAN...

1. Believes in supporting himself and his kids if he has any. He doesn't sell drugs, nor does he make excuses to not work for a living.

2. He actually has a plan for success in life, and follows it. He isn't comfortable being in the same position forever. Any man who does is a f*cking loser.

3. He is a father to his children, not just a daddy. He spends time with them, clothes, and feeds them. He never abandons, or neglects his kids.

4. A good man never beats on his woman, even if she does push him over the edge, he has the ability to walk away.

5. A good man doesn't' cheat on his wife or girlfriend,

he appreciates what he has, even if she gains weight over the years, or doesn't have the big 'ole booty. He loves her for who she is.

6. He does the little things that melts a woman's heart, like love letters, flowers, home cooked meals, massages, foreplay, walks in the park, etc.

7. He loves to show affection to his woman in front of his homies, if he don't then that's something to think about ladies...

8. He always makes eye contact when he talks to you, as well as when he listens to you talk.

9. A good man isn't cheap by any means. He is more than willing to show you a good time when he has money to spend and take you to nice places...he just doesn't want to stay cooped up in the house all the damn time either.

10. A good man respects and honors his mother, as well as God. If he doesn't have a relationship with God, then please encourage him to.

11. He realizes he isn't perfect, but he does his best to be at his best...he don't allow himself to make the same mistakes in life over and over. He learns and corrects them.

12. He loves to teach you new ideas, new concepts, and

motivates you in becoming a stronger, wiser, and more successful woman.

13. He shows his respect for you by admitting his wrongs, listening when you have something to say even if he don't want to hear it, respects your opinions, and he always treats you as his equal.

14. A good man has patience to tolerate his woman's bullsh*t, but he isn't a pushover...he'll let you know up front what he will and will NOT tolerate.

15. A good man is always down to please his woman sexually. He does whatever that makes his woman squirt, gush, scream, and shake.

16. He is educated and displays intelligence. Very important factor.

17. He doesn't go strip clubs and come home to you smelling like weed and perfume...he realizes you can strip for him for FREE.

18. He always makes time to call you during the day to see how your day going, he never goes an entire day without calling you.

19. A good man is willing to move at whatever pace that is most comfortable for YOU. he realizes a woman is very strategic with her heart...although it may become frustrating for him, he still respects you enough to match your speed.

20. A good man wrote this book…

;)

11. DO GUYS REALLY WAIT FOR SEX?

Almost every female on earth has the typical, routine, and predictable "make him wait" mentality. This bullsh*t has to stop. Little do they realize is how unrealistic that mentality is. Women feed into society's standards too much, instead of being realistic and using common sense. A HUGE reason why so many women can't keep a man, or get a man, is because they expect every guy to "wait" for them to provide sexual pleasure. Unrealistic. If you have the mentality of "only a hoe gives it up the first night" then you definitely need to study this piece. It's time to break down WHY and HOW guys DONT wait for sex. Let's get into it shall we?

DO GUYS REALLY "WAIT" FOR SEX???

Okay now ask yourself this: say you went to McDonalds and you ordered a #9 meal with a milkshake right? But they say the milkshake machine was down right?...so you say "cool"...you just substitute it for a soda right?...but they SODA machine is down also!...okay what would do you do? Do you "wait" for them to fix they soda machine and milkshake machine? NO! You're going to LEAVE and go SOMEWHERE ELSE that HAS a WORKING MILKSHAKE machine! SAME CONCEPT APPLIES TO SEX.

In the beginning, a guy doesn't know ANYTHING about you besides how you LOOK, and TALK. So by "going out" and "getting to know" each other and "talking" on the phone, that's NOT building any chemistry in the BEDROOM. Sexual chemistry is only built in the BEDROOM. NOT on the phone, or in some public place.

You ever heard the saying "what I can't get from you I can get from someone else"? You ever heard that saying? I'm sure you have. Now: do you think YOUR exempt from this saying? Don't flatter yourself.

A guy will NOT "wait" for sex with someone who is NOT his woman yet. Guys aren't stupid (some are, but most of us know what time it is) Here's the TRUTH: she's sleeping with someone already! So of course she going to make the "new guy" wait. Because she's already involved with someone! And if the guy thinks that way then you know what HE'S going to do? Get involved with someone ELSE too! Until YOUR ready to get involved with him. So what are you REALLY gaining?

If you think a guy is going to "respect" you because you made him "wait" you are a f*cking MORON. Why? Because he respects you enough to not tell you he's sleeping with someone else while he "gets to know" YOU. Good job sista! You just became an OPTION. Instead of PRIORITY. You blew it when you told him NO. Now your ass gets BENCHED for the woman who says YES. Dumb ass.

Just because a guy tries to have sex with you on the first night does NOT make him "thirsty". It just means that he's getting to the point with you. ALL people have sexual needs. Male AND female. But why should a person have to go to bed horny? And if that person DOES? Then that person is selling himself/herself short of being pleased and satisfied.

Why should a guy "wait" for something that's possibly not good? Do you "wait" for a guy to take you out? NO. If you want to go out for drinks but he says "no" do you wait for him to say yes? Or do you simply call option #2 and ask HIM out for drinks? EXACTLY.

So ladies, let's cut this "waiting game" BULLSH*T. Its tired, old, and typical. A real woman who knows what she wants shouldn't have to use her pussy as a control method to keep or get a man. A man knows INSTANTLY if he wants to wife you or one night you. So stop acting like not giving him sex is going to make him like you more. Its NOT. Use common sense ladies. It's not rocket science. Meet a guy, get laid, enjoy each other's time. Why talk to a guy you don't want to sleep with? Makes no sense. You don't know SH*T about a person until you two have sex. THATS when you see if that person is genuinely interested in you or not. Now I'm not saying sleep with every guy you meet, but why would you choose guys who you feel unsure about? Think about it.

12. REAL MEN vs. REAL N*GGAS

A REAL N**GA...

Praises his money and material over God. A "real n**ga" has no respect for women, or his mother, or his elders, or himself. A REAL N**GA has kids with multiple women, hardly takes care of any of them. If at all.

A REAL N**GA is lazy, and expects handouts in life. A REAL N**GA blames the world for his problems

A REAL N**GA will neglect you, barely take you out, never spend time with you, always puts his boys before his lady (very suspect sh*t), trap all night, or stay out all night while you at home horny and lonely, barely calls during the day because he's "busy", too manly to cuddle and watch a movie with you ("real n**gas" don't cuddle), get mad when you just want to cuddle, he never cooks for you, never washes a dish, takes you to the same restaurant as his mistress, exes, side chicks, never offer any snaps on the petro, shows no affection in public ("real n**gas" don't hold hands or kiss in public) never notices your fresh manicure, or when you shave, always too tired after work to do anything but lay-up & go to sleep, etc...

NOW...

A REAL MAN...

Praises God over money & material. A REAL MAN respects his parents, women, siblings, elders, as well as himself. A REAL MAN provides for his woman and family. A REAL MAN protects his woman with his life. A REAL MAN works hard for what he wants in life. A REAL MAN doesn't make excuses, he makes a way.

A REAL MAN WON'T neglect you, or barely take you out, or barely spend time with you, he WON'T put his boys before you (he's not suspect), or trap at all, or stay out all night, he WON'T leave you home horny and lonely, he WILL call & text during the day because he's "busy" but he not too busy for YOU, he LOVES to cuddle and watch movies (real men cuddle), he doesn't mind holding you and making you feel safe, he enjoys cooking for you, no problem washing the dishes, takes you to YOUR favorite restaurant, throws down on the petro with no problem, he enjoys affection in public because he isn't ashamed of you, he compliments your new nails, smooth legs, he's rarely too tired for his woman after work, etc.

I THINK ITS TIME TO RE-EVALUATE THE SITUATION, AND GET A GUY LIKE THIS LADIES...

REAL MEN DO EXIST.

13. 10 WAYS TO KNOW IF HE'S A GOOD MAN...OR A N*GGA

A GOOD MAN...

1. Always puts his woman first and only... he doesn't keep "female friends" around in a relationship. That's bullsh*t ladies... don't fall for it.

2. He always makes time for you even when he's with his homeboys... a simple phone call doesn't hurt.

3. He is always willing to apologize when he is wrong... no man is perfect ladies

4. He has no problem bringing you around his friends. If he don't, then he probably don't like you as much as he says...

5. He honors his mother or whatever woman that raised him...if he doesn't, then he'll never respect YOU.

43

6. He never throws his money in your face or tries to manipulate you into sex... he waits until YOUR ready and comfortable.

7. His actions always speak louder than his words. He does what he says... anything else is pure game.

8. He is educated (at least a damn GED!), independent (not trying to spend YOUR money), has a job (or at least trying), and goals.

9. He never cheats on you... if he do it once, he'll do it again...

10. He appreciates you for YOU... he never tries to make you feel bad for gaining weight, or he never compares you to another woman he desires.

Now... here's 10 ways to know if your man or the man your involved with is...

A N**GA...

1. He barely calls you. He only calls when he wants some pussy. He never calls just to talk.

2. He only comes around when you're NOT on your period...

3. He never takes you out...he wants you to always stay in the house...but he always goes out.

4. He is so-called "cool" with his "baby mamas"...but you NEVER meet them.

5. He only calls you late at night...or he says he's "too busy" to call during the day.

6. When having sex, he never looks you in the eyes. He always keeps his eyes closed...never a good sign.

7. After having sex, he gets right up and leaves...the n**ga don't even wash his balls!

8. He claims he has a "lot of female friends"...but just like #4 you NEVER meet them b*tches either...

9. He only shows affection behind closed

doors. How he treats you in public is how he REALLY feels about you. Never let him tell you different.

10. He never says "I love you" when he's around his "n**gas"...that's some sh*t to think about. He might be a "down low" brotha if you know what I mean...

So ladies, I hope I gave you some things to think about and realize from a male's perspective. And hopefully now you'll stop saying "n**gas ain't sh*t", because you'll be smart enough to leave they ass alone now...

THE TRUTH IS THE HARDEST PILL TO SWALLOW

SHANNON BRANCH

FELLAS

14. A MESSAGE TO ALL THE FELLAS

We have to stop being N**GAS, and start being MEN. We have to stop being "BABY DADDYS" and start being FATHERS. We wonder why women don't respect us, it's because we be f*cking up! You might not want to read this, but I don't give a sh*t. It needs to be said. It seems like when a man speaks the truth, n**gas get mad, and be like "man f*ck what that n**ga talking about", but turn around and listen to these dumb ass rappers who teach you how to go to jail, snitch on yourself, catch AIDS, and be fags. N**gas mess everything up for the REAL MEN out here. Every time a n**ga lie to a woman, she becomes more afraid to trust a MAN. Every time a n**ga plays games, a MAN has to pay for what YOU did. Look around you, how many men do YOU see that are fathers? Not many. How many men do YOU see who is PROUD to be in a relationship? Not many. How many husbands do YOU see who proudly claims his wife, and respects her? Not many. This HAS to change. NOW!

SOCIETY HAS NOT MAKING SH*T IMPOSSIBLE FOR US, WE ARE THE ONLY ONES MAKING THINGS HARDER FOR US!!! WE ARE DIGGING OUR OWN GRAVES!

WHY does this matter? Because we got kids out here

looking at this sh*t thinking it's cool. It's NOT. Going to the strip club every weekend is NOT cool. Laying up with different hoes who don't rrespect themselves is NOT cool. Child support is NOT cool. STDS is NOT cool. Cheating on your' girl is NOT cool. Having kids with multiple women is NOT cool. How will this change? EASY: if we start teaching each other how to be better men, and stop teaching each other dumb sh*t, and stop thinking we "players", because we all know...

The player ALWAYS gets played in the end by a
BETTER PLAYER.

That's why these hoes stay WINNING...

That's why "BABY MAMAS" are getting PAID TO HAVE KIDS...

That's why these ex-wives is laughing all the way to the bank when they're milking these sorry ass n**gas for that DIVORCE SETTLEMENT.

MY POINT IS THIS :

What one n**ga does affects the next man. And don't use "B*TCHES AIN'T SH*T" as an excuse to be an "AINT SH*T N**GA".

We have to stop hustling backwards! Let's carry ourselves like KINGS. NOT N**GAS.

And if you can't respect this chapter, then you're obviously not a REAL MAN!

15. WHAT DEFINES A TYPICAL N*GGA?

Typical n**gas are JUST like typical females: predictable. They think, say, and do the same off brand sh*t as the next corny dude. Typical males usually follow trends instead of setting them.

A typical n*gga will claim he's a "grown man" but acts like a child.

He loves bragging about how he's "getting money" but he has nothing to show for it.

Typical n*ggas stay capping on the internet. Claiming to be a "real n**ga" but his Facebook/Twitter bio is 95% lies.

He usually has kids with multiple women...and barely takes care of them. If at all.

He claims to be a "real n**ga" but wears fake jewelry.

Typical n**gas go broke and stay broke trying to

impress other broke n*ggas and hoes.

Typical n**gas love jail. They can't stay out of it.

He creates this false "playa" image to get females. Instead of being REAL and saying what's on his mind, he would rather lie to women to get what he wants.

All typical males are responsible for the typical female behavior. The male starts the cycle. The female repeats it...

He's quick to go to the strip club and is quicker to spend his cash on a thirsty stripper who cares nothing about him, but will argue his girlfriend down for asking him for money...and call her a "gold digger".

Typical n*ggas are proud tricks and ass kissers. They are the reason why so many females are entitled.

Typical n**gas always have sex with no condom. ALWAYS. Why you think so many n**gas got kids? Condoms DON'T break every time. That excuse is dead. N**gas just be going in these chicks raw.

A typical n**ga will make a baby but won't take care of it.

He has no direction in life. No plan for his future. As long as he's "getting money" right now he's satisfied.

THE TRUTH IS THE HARDEST PILL TO SWALLOW

Typical n**gas love taking pics posing with guns, smoking weed, etc. Typical males love snitching on themselves. The excuse? "I'm a real n**ga".

Typical n**gas always lying about how they got "haters". When in reality these "haters" are people who simply tells him the truth about himself.

Typical males always bragging about how many "hoes" they got. As if getting "hoes" is an achievement. Any male can pull a hoe. It's not difficult at all.

He always complains about how "b*tches ain't sh*t" but yet he never approaches women.

He thinks by having a car with rims, nice sneakers, a fresh haircut, and tattoos is going to get him a good woman. He fails to realize he's only attracting hoes and "jump-offs". Not women. Real women can care less about a n**gas rims, sneakers, etc.

He loves playing games. He constantly lies to women. He will actually have a quality female in his life but always f*cks it up by lying and being full of sh*t.

Typical males are afraid to be themselves. Or worse, they don't know how.

He will choose to sit up under his homeboys instead of his woman. And get mad when she cheats on him for a guy who actually pays attention to her.

He's always screaming "f*ck b*tches get money" but everything he does is to impress b*tches.

A typical n**ga buys into the "if she gives it up the first night she's a hoe" mentality. These morons are the ones who make women use that concept as a weapon against real men who are smart enough to not fall for that game.

Typical males are always buying the pu$$y. They will wine and dine a random chick, take her shopping, etc. but will barely take his girlfriend or wife out on a nice date...

He loves telling the next man how to manage his money when he can barely manage his own.

He usually says dumb sh*t like "I don't eat pu$$y" or "it's not cheating because we not married" or "I need a chick with some money" or some other off brand statements...

He tries way too hard to be cool. He will sell his soul for people to accept him.

Typical males never invest into anything positive or productive (art, charities, businesses, etc.) instead he will spend all his money on weed, alcohol, hoes, and clothes. Things that does nothing for them

He gossips about other guys. Or discusses what's in the next man's pockets.

THE TRUTH IS THE HARDEST PILL TO SWALLOW

Typical males can't handle rejection. His ego and pride is so big that if a woman turns him down she goes from being a (insert complimentary name here) to a B*TCH, or a "hoe" for not giving him the time of day.

Typical males are T-H-I-R-S-T-Y. They have no standards. They will have sex with any female. No matter how she looks, thinks, smells, etc.

A typical n**ga is probably YOU...or someone you know of...or someone your currently involved with. Either way, typical males and n**gas are the WORST. They will generate nothing but problems and headaches for you ultimately resulting in a complete waste of your time. Typical n**gas come in various shapes, sizes, and colors, but the SAME mentality. Stay away from these losers. They may look and pretend to be "real men", but these chameleons will get you nowhere in life.

So ladies make sure your man has NONE of these traits or you can forget about that thing called marriage. And fellas make sure YOU don't have any of these traits, or you will forever be passed up by real women, and will forever be laughed at by real men.

SHANNON BRANCH

16. THE REASON WHY WOMEN
PLAY GAMES

Okay fellas, I know y'all probably sick of the games, lies, and bullsh*t with these females right? I know you to the point where you starting to feel like you'll NEVER meet or find a sista who isn't stuck on stupid right? Well, don't feel alone! Me as a single brotha I know how you feel bruh, frustrated, tired, and irritated with women with their twisted, warped, immature shenanigans. So how do us men cope with the corny, childish, lame, and fake, off brand behavior that these ladies display? This is where I get totally confused as well...but hell, I'm a man just like you are. But I'll do my best to help us brothas out...I mean, we do got to stick together right?

First off fellas, here's where I think we go wrong at. Women aren't really sure about what they want when they first meet us. You know why? Because their unsure of who WE are! Women are very self-protective of themselves, meaning that they put on this armor like Teflon that prevents men from penetrating their hearts, minds, and bodies, because a woman's heart, mind, and body is like a man's money. Something that's hard to get. So how do we infiltrate? Simple: We have to build a woman's trust. How do we do that? Well my man, that depends on what type of female it is.

Some women are easy to get with, and some aren't. It's all about who you choose. But the bottom line is, a woman protects their mind, body, and heart from a man until she feels comfortable. Or at least she tries to. Some of us brothas are just irresistible. See, in the beginning women will tend to test us just to see what type of person we are. A woman's first reaction when being approached by a man is usually negative. Whether he's sexy to her or not. Real talk. You know why? Because MEN usually play games, so a woman has to play games as well, just to feel comfortable in knowing if this man approaching her is either trying to be that handsome, prince charming brotha who she'll bring home to mom, or if he's some sick pervert who likes to sniff a woman's underwear after she works out for 2 hours. See my drift? Women have to feel secure, and playing games is simply a woman's way of doing that. Its corny but hey, its their comfort zone. It protects them. At least in their mind.

Now, I know you probably saying to yourself "awww this n**ga taking up for these b*tches" right? Well actually, all I'm doing is showing my fellas why these females play these games they play. But why do we keep getting caught up in a woman's scam? Because we don't do our homework on these females! Soon as we see a pretty face or a phat ass, we ready to leave our baby mamas! Well not me, I don't have any kids...but you dig what I'm saying right? Ladies are approached 100 times a f*cking day!

So picture this fellas: If the tables were turned, and women approached us men instead of us men approaching women, then we'll see why females be on some anti-social, wishy washy mess! It gets irritating after a while when a woman goes to the grocery store and EVERY male in the ENTIRE store is trying to holla. And think about this too fellas: Women are afraid to say "no" to a man nowadays because so many brothas flip out and react violently. So its hard for a woman to keep it "real". It lightweight makes sense. Or maybe just to me because I've studied females for so long that I can finish a lot of these chicks sentences........damn I'm good.

Anyways, the truth is fellas, is that women don't really know how to handle all the attention they get. So out of human character, a woman is most likely to make a bad choice when offered so many choices. its reality guys. It sucks too! Because we all feel like we're the realest, best thing to come into that woman's life right? Well think about this: the WOMAN doesn't know that! She isn't used to every man being Casanova, so automatically she's thinking in her head "this n**ga probably got 4 baby mamas", while we all up in her face thinking in OUR head "yeah she wants to f*ck", see my point? So we have to give our ladies a LITTLE credit!

Now granted guys, there ARE A LOT of young sistas(old ones too) who is on some straight up BULLSH*T! But see, I'm going to save that topic for later, that way we can attack them little girls who get a kick out of being full of games just because. I got something special for they ass, trust me fellas, don't worry. But until that memorable moment comes, understand that a lot of our women don't play games just because, they have their reasons fellas, even if we don't understand it or agree with it. I sure don't...but hey, I'm a dude, I'm not supposed to right?

17. REAL WOMEN vs. FAKE B*TCHES

Ever since I was a child I always expressed myself in the most brutally honest, and creative way. Whether it was through my drawings, paintings, music, or my writing, I always displayed my views, thoughts, and feelings with no shame or fear of being vulnerable to the world or trying to put on a front to be accepted. I'm too thorough for that. And that's what makes a real man. A real man has his own identity. Not trying to fit in with the world and is never afraid to be himself. A real man knows the difference between reality and illusion and never allows society's illusions become his reality.

But what makes a real WOMAN?...some of the values I stated above right?...well if that's all it took to be classified as a "real man/woman" then we would ALL be "real" right? and there would be NO fake people right? Let's be "real" here, EVERYONE claims they so "real" right?...but NO one admits to being fake.....THIS is where the problem lies...too many fake b*tches claiming to be "real women", and too many fake n**gas claiming to be real men...but in this segment we're gonna get intense (you know how I do it) and speak directly to the real women out here...and the fake.

A REAL WOMAN...

1.   Overstands that having her own money, her own car, her own place (apartment, house, condo, etc.) does NOT make her a real woman. She knows she must carry herself in a manner that demands respect from anyone surrounding her...there's plenty of females out here who got Benzes, houses, and great credit...but also has the concept of life all f*cked up.

2.   A real woman never depends on no man for anything. She is willing to arm-wrestle a man on a date at the dinner table over whose going to cover the tab or she is infamous for turning down gifts because she isn't into men buying her attention or interest...plus she doesn't like random men spending money on her...just because he "offered", a real woman still refuse to accept. She was raised better than that.

3.   She takes care of her kids the best way she can with or without the father. She puts her child/children first and never neglects or abandons them.

4.   A real woman don't date, "talk to", or f*ck multiple men whether she single or not. She has more class than that...and she don't use the "I'm single" line as an excuse...she has more productive things to do in her life than keep a team of men. She prefers to date, "talk to", and f*ck ONE at a time. Only bops juggle. Period.

5.   She don't dress like a slut and get offended when she is approached like one. She knows how to dress like a lady and still get the same attention...matter of fact what kind of woman wants attention from a bunch of guys anyways?...think about it.

6.   She keeps successful, productive, and goal oriented people in her circle. A real woman never hangs with

lowlifes...Like the saying goes "birds don't fly with eagles and peacocks don't stroll with chickens".

7. Only a real woman admits her wrongs and is willing to improve herself for the better. Mentally, physically, emotionally, and spiritually.

8. When a real woman has a man in her life she gives him her ALL. Not some. Any chick with a pussy can get a man, but only a real woman knows how to keep one.

9. She doesn't use her pussy as leverage to get ahead in life. She's too intelligent for that, so she uses her mind instead.

10. She doesn't give her number out to a dude she not interested in just to ignore his calls later...nor do she add or accept random dudes on MySpace/Facebook for no reason...nor do she stay in a relationship with a man who treats her right just to cheat with a "n**ga" who treat her like a slut...nor do she argue with other females she don't know over the internet...nor do she fight over a dude...nor do she "go out" every f*cking weekend...I could go on forever about what makes a real woman...but I'll give you 10...so now it's time to break down 10 things about...

A FAKE B*TCH...

1. Looks, talks, walks, dresses, f*cks, eats, sh*ts, sleeps, and breathes like a real woman...the only difference

is the mentality.

2. A fake ass b*tch always gets mad and be ready to fight when someone calls her a "fake ass b*tch"... think about WHY he/she called you a fake b*tch...he/she didn't call you that for nothing. But once again, every fake b*tch claims and manipulates herself into believing she is a real woman...so when someone shows her a mirror of who she really is she ready to take off her rings and heels. A real woman would never be called a fake b*tch. Think about it.

3. A fake b*tch always talk that "I don't need no man" bullsh*t...that saying was created to give women confidence in themselves and not be so dependent on a man...nothing more, nothing less. But fake b*tches really believe she "don't need no man"...but everything she does is for a man. Think about THAT.

4. She fails to realize that getting random negative attention is going to get her NOWWHERE in life...but pregnant, infected with a STD, stalked, verbally abused, beaten, lied to, misled, raped, or even killed...

5. A fake b*tch goes to the club with no money...and have the nerve to call the next chick or a dude broke...she wears her best friends clothes to the club...but hate on what the next chick is wearing...she sits down the entire night...but say "I'm bored"...she accepts drinks from a stranger but acts stuck up towards him...and she always talk that "I'm independent" bullsh*t...but don't own a damn thing.

6. She likes to play men. It builds her confidence and
    self-esteem that she can pull off a great lie and never
    get caught...she loves having men chasing after her,
    she craves attention from a bunch of dudes in the
    club, Facebook, MySpace, etc. She can't stand being
    alone. She needs someone to notice her so she can
    feel important. She calls multiple guys to keep from
    being bored instead of calling ONE guy to have a
    meaningful conversation. She even has sex with
    guys she don't even like to keep from being bored
    instead of making love to a man who will cherish
    her for the rest of her life.

7. She says full of sh*t lines like... "I have a lot of male
    friends"...or "I never did this before with any
    guy"...or "I don't know you like that"...or "I don't
    have sex with just anybody"...or "I'm just looking
    for friends"...or "I don't give out my number but I'll
    take yours"...or "I been busy"...or "I fell asleep"...or
    "I just met you"...or "I only slept with like..."

8. Fake b*tches come on Facebook with no purpose
    but to comment on a bunch of random dudes she
    don't even know pages and photos...request random
    dudes for no reason...accept random dudes for no
    reason...give her number out to random dudes for
    no reason...pose half naked in 50% of her
    pictures...has over 1,000 photos, does nothing
    productive on Facebook but "talk to my
    friends"(b*tch please)...has over 1,000 friends and
    she only knows no more than 10 of them
    personally...her top friends is a bunch of dudes that
    she so called "grew up with"...is always online but
    always talk about how "busy" she is...and loves to
    call a dude thirsty if he say two words to her corny

ass...

9. She gives out fake numbers...she plays on peoples phones...she lies about her age...she lies about what she has, does, likes, dislikes, and wants. She claims wants a good man but act as if she wants a "n**ga" when she gets a good man.

10. A fake b*tch loves to call a dude a "stalker" for calling her phone after she told him to "call me back" instead of "leave me alone". A fake b*tch will pretend to also like the same dude just to get free meals, outfits, gifts, or any other form of gain. She will then tell the ole dude she just f*cked and sucked, "I'm not ready to be in a relationship"...but days later she got a man.

A fake ass b*tch is probably YOUR' ass or somebody you know very well. Or it can be a chick you dealing with right now, or a broad you just slept with and left alone because she may have fit into one of these 10 above, but there's really a million ways to detect a fake b*tch...but like I mentioned above for the REAL WOMEN I only decided to list 10.

18. THE REASON WHY WOMEN LIE MORE THAN MEN

Like the saying goes: "men lie, women lie, but numbers don't". But there's one thing that nobody ever mentions: is who lies MORE. Now I'm sure if you're a female reading this your already uptight, your face is scrunched up, and you probably thinking this is some "woman bashing" piece right? WRONG. This piece is to open a lot of people's eyes about how GOOD women lie, and WHY they lie. Mainly because society has given women no choice. Every day there's some unwritten law being passed that its bad if a woman does this, or does that. So women lie to protect themselves from being exposed, ridiculed, and embarrassed. Can you blame them?

For the guys reading this I want you to understand that I'm not defending women being liars. Put yourself in a woman's shoes. Not literally...but you know what I mean. Think about how difficult it is being a woman in today's society where every move a woman makes is being judged. Women can't leave their homes without being critiqued on how they look, dress, smell, etc. This same endless stereotyping goes for what women do. Women are constantly told how to look, act, dress, talk, feel, etc. they forget how to be THEMSELVES. So they usually put on some image or facade to look a certain way. The same thing applies to her actions. If she goes to the club and meets a guy, and wants to go home with him, she probably will. But will she tell all her friends about it? Probably not. Some do, but the ones who got a little bit of class usually don't. If her friends ask if she let him "hit it" you think she's going to say yes? Hells the f*ck no. The last thing women want is they own friends calling her a "hoe".

The reason why women lie more than men is simple: men don't give a f*ck about getting caught. Men also don't care about being called a hoe. If a guy meets a girl and decides to sleep with her instantly, it won't make him look bad at all. If he tells all his friends how he met some chick at the club and he smashed in the parking lot, all his boys is going to praise him. Well this is the opposite for females. Women are FORCED to hide they dirt. If a woman tells her father, brother, or best friend how she let 3 guys bust big fat nuts on her face last night do you think she's about get a high five?! Nope, she's about to get a 100-Hand E. Honda slap instead.

The bottom line is this: if a woman cheats, she HAS to cover it up, because at the end of the day she has to maintain her "image" (in her mind). ALL females feel like they every move is being observed. Even behind closed doors. That's why you always hear a woman say "I never did this before" RIGHT before she's about to suck you off in your car. That's why women always tell guys they only slept with LIKE before spewing out the actual number...which is ALWAYS under 10. Women are called hoes, sluts, b*tches, and bops ALL DAY LONG no matter HOW truthful and honest they are, so women spend more time trying to avoid these stereotypes and cover they dirt they feel FORCED to lie.

Do I support women who lie? No. But do I understand WHY they lie? OF COURSE.

19. WHAT EXACTLY DEFINES A "GOOD WOMAN"?

Okay let's be honest here y'all, have you ever met anyone who told you that they are fake and full of sh*t? I seriously doubt it. We all feel in our mind and heart that we're so-called "real" and "good people" right? Simply because we can't observe ourselves like someone else can. And we tend to ignore and not see the traits that makes us human...flaws. And no one is perfect, but there are just some traits and habits that are just totally unacceptable, especially for females. And truthfully, I don't think females nowadays even know what a "good woman" really is, or better yet what it takes to be a "good woman"...so I figure i take the time to show those who claim they are...but really isn't. As well as give the true "good women" out there a checklist. But what exactly defines a "good woman"?

I'll break it down for you...

A GOOD WOMAN...

1. Always handles her business. She never puts partying, clubbing, sex, etc. before her priorities such as school, work, bills, her kids, etc.

2. She overstands the concept of 50/50. A woman

must be able and willing to match what she demands from the other half. Period.

3. A good woman respects herself, and gives everyone around her a reason to respect her as well...not just because she's a "female". She EARNS respect.

4. She don't go clubbing every weekend, or has a "lot of male friends". This type of scumbag mentality is only trapped inside the mind of bops...or typical females...but a good woman sees reality...unlike most females.

5. Never will a good woman "keep her options open" in the same breath of saying "I want a good man". These types of b*tches can't be taken seriously at all. They not willing to give one man her all. Never a good thing.

6. She don't have a billion men on her friend list on MySpace or Facebook...unless she is a celebrity, model, artist, etc...if she isn't, then how does she know all of these clowns? think about it...

7. Her top friends doesn't mainly consist of men with their shirt off.

8. She doesn't say dumb sh*t like..."I don't really hang with females, most of my friends are guys".

9. Independent is a very important word when defining a "good woman". She spends her OWN

money...not everyone else's.

10. She don't still kick it with her "exes"...this is pure bullsh*t ladies, so please stop trying to convince us men that it's not, okay?

11. She keeps her word and realizes that actions speak louder than words. She doesn't say she's gonna do something and don't do it...these are the epitome of bull- sh*tters.

12. She always puts her kids first. She doesn't leave them over "auntie's" house every weekend while she go out. If you got kids, that clubbing sh*t is over sweetie. It's time to grow up. Flat out.

13. If she is married, or in a relationship, she isn't on Social Media still "looking for friends". C'mon now, let's be real.

14. She has goals, hobbies (going out isn't a hobby ladies), has common sense (a degree doesn't qualify), and works towards bettering herself...not talking that "I'm 'bout to do this and do that"...what are you doing NOW?

15. A good woman has god in her life. if she is atheist, she has good intentions for herself, her life, and those around her...but she'll eventually find god.

16. She understands that money doesn't define success...any female who doesn't will more than

likely do anything to get it. A good woman don't sacrifice her self-worth for financial gain.

17. She doesn't date "thugs" or "street n*ggas*. She only gives the time of day to a man who puts her first and only and has a legitimate hustle.

18. She isn't into playing games like most females. She knows what she wants, and earns it respectfully. Not by trying to manipulate men/women (whatever she prefers) into getting it.

19. She has a good relationship with her mother or father, or BOTH. At least with someone who has raised her right. most women haven't been. That's why there's so many bops and sluts out here.

20. A good woman recognizes her worth. She overstands that she's a QUEEN. Nothing less.

20. THE TRUTH ABOUT WOMEN WITH MALE FRIENDS

To every guy reading this I encourage you to share this piece with your homeboys. You might already be up on game, but if you're not keep reading. To the ladies reading this I hope you learn something from this piece also. I'm gonna touch on all aspects of the "male friends" concept, while revealing a few secrets on why so many guys play along with this GAME. Secrets that a lot of women obviously DONT know...

Now if you are already turning your nose up from reading this then I don't know whether to feel sorry for you for being so damn stubborn and blind to the obvious truth, or to laugh at you for allowing a woman to brainwash you into believing she REALLY has "male friends". This is why you need to keep reading. You obviously haven't studied the game, neither have you realized you've been getting played like a SUCKA for a long time now. To the fellas who play along with the "male friend" game, hats off to you, because you make it work to your advantage...but for the chumps who are blind and keep believing women have "male friends" for the sole purpose of true benevolence and nothing more, you need to read this piece 100 times a day until you memorize what I'm about to teach you. Pay attention!

I know you met plenty of women who told you all of her male friends are guys she "grew up with", or "known since high school", or how "they are like brothers", and a bunch of other reasons right? And just like a moron, you BELIEVED her. This is where ALL men f*ck up. We must realize that women will ALWAYS be more clever than men, why? Because women are MASTERS of illusion. Why you think it's so hard to catch a woman cheating? Or lying? Or playing you? Think about it. The same goes for these "male friends". Don't be stupid. Use common sense. What do you think she REALLY has "male friends" for? To play basketball with? To talk about lingerie with? To watch football with? F*CK OUTTA HERE

Here's the REAL truth...

THERE IS NO SUCH THING AS MALE FRIENDS!!!

There's only 3 types of dudes women keep around... Only Clutch buddies, F*ck buddies, and ATM buddies...

I will break down all three for you...

THE CLUTCH BUDDY (The attention giver)

This is the guy who hangs out with her from time to time, she tells you her problems, you call or text her late at night, or she calls or texts you late at night to see "what you doing". She lets you believe she's waiting for the right one, she gives you the window of opportunity by telling you she likes to "take things slow" and "get to know someone before jumping into a relationship". You think she REALLY cares about how your day is going? Or how you feel? She might. But she REALLY only calls you when she's BORED dude. Simple as that.

She will add you to her list of "attention givers" and call or text you because she know she can get your attention when she wants it. Women LOVE to feel important, and the "clutch" buddy: meaning "guy she can always turn to for an ego boost" is always there to gas her up. Either by reminding her she's beautiful, or boosting her self-esteem by taking her out, or listening to her vent when her boyfriend is treating her wrong, or by simply answering her phone calls when she "needs someone to talk to". the "clutch" buddy is always right there.

Now this is where it gets tricky...a LOT of men already know this, and they use it to their advantage. For example: a guy who knows the game will play along and ACT like he's really trying to be her "friend", but he's really using her to get attention from OTHER women. How? If a guy walks into a restaurant, bar, club, or any public place with a nice looking woman...or two...or three...all the women around will think he's intriguing because he has a nice looking woman or a few nice looking women around him. Women are honestly intimidated by other attractive women.

Why do you think they compete so hard to stand out amongst other women? Another example is a guy who will have "female friends" for the benefit of getting with one of HER friends, or even getting advice on HOW to get with one of her friends...or better yet HER. But she so busy thinking he's trying to be her "homeboy" she don't even know she's being GAMED. The guy who knows most of her deepest thoughts and secrets is usually the guy she ends up marrying...or f*cking. Like all women say: "gotta be friends first". This leads to the next type of "male friend" she keeps around...

THE F*CK BUDDY (a.k.a. "best friend")

You probably either played this role, or been PLAYED by this role. Women will tell you anything if you let her. When she says "he's like my brother, we known each other for years" do you REALLY believe that this guy just appeared in her life and NEVER got a piece of that ass? C'mon son. Open your eyes.

How many times have YOU smashed a chick who has a boyfriend, fiancé, or a husband?...and if her man asks her about YOU what do you think she tells him?

The SAME thing she told YOU about that OTHER mysterious guy who be calling her...

The cool thing about this is that both sides usually know the deal, so in the end there's no feelings hurt. Only a fool will consider "wifing" up a chick who lets a guy smash casually. You think she won't play you for a SMOOTHER guy who has MORE money and more status? WAKE UP!!!!

If you get the benefit of blazing a chick without having to commit that's like being selected to receive a free Ferrari via email. It's some BULLSH*T.

Hit it once and keep it moving. That's how real "playas" do right? WRONG.

Most dudes keep smashing a "jump-off" until he gets her knocked, or caught up in some drama, or until he loses his respect or luster and gets dropped.

YOU as the man have to ALWAYS drop the chick. Don't EVER get dropped. EVER. Hit it once and keep it moving. ALWAYS.

THE ATM BUDDY (The Trick)

Almost every woman who is physically attractive (not you boo boo please sit down. thanks) always have a guy around who don't mind spending a little cash for her entertainment. Whether it's to go hang out, go out to eat, catch a movie, go clubbing together, and shopping...hell even exquisite trips and cruises.

Some guys just got cash flow like that, and he might not mind spending on a woman. These are the ULTIMATE suckas to women...a woman MIGHT let the dude smash, but usually she leads him on to thinking he has a chance with her, so she might seduce him by telling him what he wants to hear, or by even giving him some "Becky" in the front seat of his Beamer, Benz, or Bentley, but in the end...she gets what SHE wants. MONEY, TRIPS, ATTENTION, and GIFTS.

Now...if you can't see by now that you been either getting played, or simply playing yourself, then you need to go and re-read this piece another 100 times. If you dealing with a woman who claims to have "male friends" remember what I told you:

WOMEN DONT KEEP FRIENDS, ONLY
CLUTCH, F*CK, AND ATM BUDDIES!!!!

And ladies...if you STILL attempt to run this game on

your boyfriend, or the current guy you're dating,

DO NOT LET HIM SEE THIS CHAPTER! YOU KNOW ITS TRUE!

CUT THE BULLSH*T!!!

21. INSECURE GUYS

Nothing is worse than hooking up with a sexy, cool, down to earth chick just to find out she has a controlling, insecure, cock blocking, jealous ass boyfriend. Guys have to realize that women can't be controlled. ALL women choose.

Women are approached by men ALL day EVERY day, and if she respects you then she won't cheat or creep on you. A lot of dudes fail to realize the more you cuff a chick the more she'll want to stray away. I see so many dudes out here with quality women, but have no clue on how to KEEP them. They think by smothering her, buying her things 24/7, and cuffing her is going to keep her around. When in reality cuffing is the quickest way to lose a woman.

NO woman wants to be controlled. Women want freedom and space just like men do. I see so much cuffing going on out here it's sickening. And it needs to stop. Seriously. It's disgusting when a man tries to confront another man for smashing his girl. Or catches feelings because she messes with another guy. If she cheats on you then she doesn't care about your feelings. Take it like a G and move on. She was probably a hood rat when you met her anyway. You just didn't pay attention to the obvious red flags.

I get sick and tired of dudes cuffing hoes they just met. If you only been kicking it with the chick for a few weeks and you already on Facebook putting "in a relationship" as your status then you playing yourself.

Let HER choose YOU. ALL females have options. As well as GAME. So stop pursuing these chicks! I also notice how so many cats be cuffing these females in the club and at parties. SHE'S NOT YOUR GIRL!

If she gave you her # keep it moving! Do NOT sit up under the broad all night talking her ear off! You think you're the only guy who got her number that night? Nah G.

Fellas we have to do better.

Every now and then I get inbox messages on Facebook from dudes asking for advice about their girl, what they should do, and how he can't get her to stop bopping. Or even worse, some goof inboxing me trying to check ME for smashing HIS girl. First off, how am I supposed to know she had a man?

SHE DIDN'T MENTION YOU PLAYBOY!

And if she did, but I ended up smashing anyway, then that tells you how important you are to her.

SHE DOESN'T RESPECT YOU!

Threatening another dude through twitter/Facebook? for smashing your girl? L-A-M-E!!! Guys need to start thinking before acting. Exposing a weak pimp hand by checking another man for f*cking YOUR chick is the worst move. You need to check your' B*TCH.

If you got a girl and she creeps on you, don't show emotion! Yeah it's going to hurt, but don't let HER know! It's simple...

REPLACE HER WITH BETTER AND KEEP IT MOVING.

Why would you get all emotional over a chick who visibly don't respect you OR your feelings? Dudes need to stop getting attached to these chicks. A woman will ALWAYS choose. No matter how good you are to her. Always remember: PUSSY TURNS 18 EVERY DAY, so don't spend a SECOND worrying about ONE chick when there's MILLIONS of women on earth. It don't matter how attractive she is. Or how much money she got, or how great her pu$$y is.

THERE'S ALWAYS BETTER.

Be a man of means, always display confidence, and be QUICK to replace a b*tch if she don't play her cards right.

OUTRO

22. IS BEING SINGLE BETTER NOWADAYS?

Everywhere you turn you always see some couple walking around holding hands, or you log on Facebook and your homepage is blown up with statuses from online friends bragging about they "boo", or how they so in love...just to see days later that same person's next status is "now single". It seems like everybody wants to be in love, but very few people have what it takes to make a relationship last forever.

Every female thinks she's "wifey" material. Every dude claims to be a "good man". Every hoe wants to be saved, and every n**ga wants a mainline. Relationships nowadays are a complete joke. Mainly because very few people take it serious. Let alone even relationship material. Relationships today seem to be more for show and tell, instead of for true love and loyalty.

THINK ABOUT THIS...

1. How much money, time, and progress have you lost due to relationships?

2. Does your partner contribute to your career goals?

3.   How many advancement opportunities have you passed up?

4.   Are you satisfied with your current living situation?

I personally believe being single is much better than being committed nowadays. Probably because I realize it's nearly impossible for people to be loyal to one person. The days when two people can focus completely on each other and remain loyal forever are gone. Escaping temptation in today's world is almost unrealistic. Internet dating sites, social networking sites, clubs, parties, the new age concept of "friends", media outlets, peer pressure, etc. make trusting someone with your heart and faith very difficult.

Women nowadays think like guys. They want to do what guys do. When it comes to women, the more attractive, desired, credible, and established she is, the less faithful and honest she is. Why? Because she holds position of power given to her by men. She has the power to choose. AND she has a "image" or "reputation" to maintain (in her mind). So many guys base a woman's value off of her looks, opposed to her mind. Same goes for us males. We lie too. A lot. The more confident, paid, established, and powerful we are in society, the less we focus on one woman. It is what is. Most men have a team of chicks. Women too. They keep a team of guys for every occasion. Thinking this will change once your "in a relationship" is not smart thinking.

This is why so many hearts and feelings get hurt. NO woman OR man will admit to being a schemer, gamer, a cheater, or a bull-sh*tter.

We all are selfish. Honestly. We think about SELF in relationships (how is this beneficial for me? what's in it for me?) I feel if you ready to settle down, get married, and have children with your partner, then yes a serious relationship is a good move. But if you rather kick it every other weekend, go out with your friends, you still in the party/club scene, you don't like being questioned, then you're better off single.

Even if you more of a chill type person, if you rather have the option to deal with a person if you choose to, instead of an obligation, then being dolo is always better. Many people want to be in love so bad they end up settling for someone they always end up regretting later. Why waste time doing this?

Look at the summer. EVERYBODY is "now single" right?

Look at the winter. EVERYBODY is "now in a relationship" right?

Let's be real: EVERY woman claims to be "wifey" material.

EVERY guy claims to be a "good man".

Once again, NO person will admit to being full of sh*t...

I've been single for years. By preference. And I feel GREAT. I do what I want, when I want, how I want. Not having to answer to no broad. I can deal with chicks on my own terms while not being obligated to anyone. That is a liberating feeling, being able to do as you please with nothing or no one keeping tabs on your every move or thinking they control you. Having freedom is 100 times better than being on a leash. And it's not like I can't get a girlfriend. I'm just too smart for that bullsh*t. Relationships are an anchor to progression in life. So many people rely on relationships to progress. And end up broke/miserable trying to keep the other person happy. I was one of those guys who always had to have a female up under me in order to feel complete. I had to snap outta that bullsh*t. I look back on every female I ever dealt with, and I have nothing to show for it today, but worthless memories. Relationships come and go.

The only females who will be loyal to just any guy is fat, desperate, broke, ugly b*tches who either got low self-esteem, or don't pull many guys. So they take what they can get. Now there are a LOT of beautiful women who also have low self-esteem. It's sad. I see so many beautiful women wasting time and money trying to keep some guy, or chasing some guy, and losing focus of SELF. This world is about SELF. You have to be in love with yourself first before you can be in love with someone else. We live in a selfish, self-centered, capitalist world, and it's rare that a person will consider your well-being and feelings before his/her own. This is why you should NEVER get attached to fakes. Men make fatal mistakes by getting attached to almost any women. Women make fatal mistakes by getting attached to the wrong men. PEOPLE ARE USERS. Have fun with him/her, enjoy his/her company, but :

DO NOT GET EASILY ATTACHED...EVER.

FELLAS

When you're broke, NO woman wants you. So trying to maintain a relationship with limited funds is a disaster waiting to happen. Don't let women gas you up by saying "money isn't everything". "I don't need a man for his money, I got my own". She saying that to YOU, to make you feel better. Does she really mean it? Go broke or STAY broke and watch how fast she loses interest.

Tony Montana said it best:

"first you get the money, then you get the power, then you get the woman"

LADIES

Stop dreaming. If you don't like giving head, you're gonna get cheated on. If you don't like cooking, you're gonna get cheated on. If you think porn is "gross", you're probably gonna get cheated on. 9 times out of 10, if you do everything your man wants, your still gonna get cheated on. Now: if you don't mind the fact that your just the "mainline" and your man has other options, then you will be able to succeed in a relationship. But expecting your man to NEVER touch another pussy after you?

STOP DREAMING.

You see so many people say "I'm focused on me" after they break up with someone. But why wait until you break up with someone to focus on yourself? That should be an everyday thing right? The bottom line is: relationships are a waste of time if you're not ready to get married and have children.

Having a girlfriend/boyfriend, Playing house, living together, helping raise somebody else's kids, being committed to someone with no ring, is CORNY.

I rather deal with someone if I CHOOSE to. If she get on my nerves then I simply replace her with better, With no remorse or feelings about it. I wish relationships was like back in the days when our grandparents were kids, but it's not anymore. We live in the "playa" era. Everybody wants to have "friends", "options", and a "team". So therefore I rather remain single. That way, I'm always ahead of the game. But that's just me though.

23. WORDS OF ENCOURAGEMENT TO SINGLE MOTHERS

I'm speaking to all the single mothers out there. To the strong, determined, focused women out there who have children, and you raise them on your own the best way that you can, just know that you'll be blessed for your endless pain, struggle, and efforts. To all the sistas who cannot afford college because you have to pay for a babysitter in order to work just to make ends meet, don't ever give up. I pass these words of encouragement onto any woman who has a child or children, or who is expecting.

I know it's extremely hard to deal with the fact that the child's father may have up and left, or he is unfit to be around your child or children, but you cannot allow your personal emotions keep your child from having a father. If the man responsible for that child is unable to come around for whatever reasons, then take the initiative and find a way to make it work, because that child needs a dad. If child support is the only option, then so be it. But keeping the father away for your own personal preference is downright selfish.

People do change, sometimes for the better, and sometimes for the worse. But at the end of the day, you have a responsibility, and that's to be there for that child whether the father is present or not.

I see a lot of beautiful young ladies out here who have

no choice but to quit their jobs, drop out of high school, turn to prostitution, just to be there for those kids. You have to continue to push yourself into being that child's mother, AND his or her father if need be. In my honest opinion, a woman should be married and well established in her career and finances before having kids, but we all know that's easier said than done.

So if you're single, and you have a child, then make sure the man who you bring into your life from now on is an example of what you would want your son to be when he grows up. Don't get with a man just because he can take care of you financially, or because he got a big dick, or he's a baller, because it's no longer about just you, your child needs a father. Period. And your child comes first. Period. You come second.

To all the ladies who have children but still want to bop around, mess with dudes, and go out and run the streets, it's time to snap out that bullsh*t. Think about how you would feel if your mommy left you over somebody else's house and you don't see her until the next day. It's cool to get out and enjoy yourself every now and then, but if you spend more time going out "looking cute", getting "throwed" in the club, or smoking weed then spending time with your kids, you're not being an example for that child. All those club hopping days are long gone sista. It's time to grow up. Now. You must stay away from the things that keeps us off track.

We've all experienced growing up without something. But nothing is worse than having a mother who isn't in our lives, so treat your child like you would want to be treated if you were still a child.

That means putting your child before anything, including men, kicking it, and going out. If you feel bitter about men because of the child's father, just know that there are a lot of men out here who would love to be a role model for your children.

Good men are out here. Never hold grudges towards the next man you meet, because he could be the one to lead your son or daughter into the right direction.

And know that you are still the same beautiful young woman who you were before you brought that gift into this world.

God puts us all through pain in order to handle the happiness and blessings that's bound to come. So do not get discouraged ladies, keep striving to better yourself, and never feel unwanted, or unattractive, because a mother is the EPITOME of beauty.

24. HOW TO RECOGNIZE & LEARN YOUR SELF WORTH

So many of us want love, commitment, honesty, trust, loyalty, excitement, but very few of us know how to go about it. We often put ourselves in situations that are toxic for our personal growth. We often sacrifice our health (mental & physical) for temporary gratification. This must stop. None of us are getting any younger, and it's time we start learning how to value our time, as well as ourselves. Recognizing & learning self-worth takes a lot of effort, no matter who you are, because we all find ourselves settling for things and people that don't contribute to our well-being. But WHY is the question?

Well, some of us feel we will find what we want by making exceptions. This is where a LOT of us go wrong. We waste years, months, weeks, days, MINUTES on people who we already know isn't right for us. I see so many ladies being in exclusive relationships with men that don't have half the requirements of a worthy mate. Let alone being her choice.

Same goes for the guys, I see a lot of young men taking on the responsibility of raising another man's kids, that the mother is still seeing from time to time. We find ourselves in predicaments that only causes problems for us. So HOW do we identity our worth, and HOW do we weed out the ones who only take us for granted, or treats us less than what we TRULY are: KINGS & QUEENS. If we view ourselves as anything less, then we will never get treated how we truly want, because we set our standards too low. A person can only treat you how you allow them to.

Self-esteem is an issue for many women as well men; and in these days. Television, Media, Internet, Magazines, Movies, peer pressure, etc. (society) brainwashes women into believing they have to be this ultra-thin model, or have this type of hair, this type of body, this type of personality, to be beautiful.

What is surprising is how quick we are to accept another person's judgment and how serious our lack of faith in ourselves can become. No person or people can determine your worth. YOU determine your worth.

Look at yourself as a BUSINESS. Meaning, your time equals MONEY. You are a personal establishment. So you can control who you bring into your circle of business.

Everyone you associate with has some form of effect on you, so it's very important that you choose your circle very wisely, because who you bring around you can help you or hurt you. Stop wasting your time with unqualified people.

Personally, I've reached a point in my life where I had to fall back from a lot of things, a lot of people, and just get myself right. At the end of the day we all have real situations and real lives, but we rarely focus on that because we too busy trying to keep up with what's going on in the outside world. As well as trying to make others happy, but deep down we're not being fulfilled.

I had to once detach myself from everything for a while. Now I'm back. More positive, spiritual, focused, and more determined than I ever been.

My whole aura is upgraded now. New and improved. I had to let go of all the pain, anger, hurt, and frustration that was inside my heart. I had to heal, instead of trying to cope with life with a scarred heart, mind, and soul. I had to fix myself.

I got ULTRA focused.

I'm blessed to be healthy, handsome, educated, single, no children, and determined to be successful in life. I refuse to let anything or anyone intervene with my focus now. I only focus on things that are going to help me be successful.

I no longer entertain bullsh*t. I no longer associate with shady friends and fake family. I encourage you all to take time and do soul searching, as well as evaluating your surroundings before you dedicate your time and energy to anyone or anything in life. Happiness starts within.

Once you achieve self-happiness, identity your self-worth, then everything else you desire in life will fall in place.

25. LAST WORDS

I would like to say I'm blessed, humbled, and grateful for everyone who purchased this book. As well as everyone who has followed me, showed me love, supported my art, and kept up with my posts on Social Media over the years.

I'm thankful for ALL the people who call me, inbox me, and email me for advice with relationships, dating, self-esteem, self-worth, depression, life, etc...

I'm thankful for ALL the people who I helped through difficult times. I know what it feels like to struggle. I know what it feels like to struggle with life, love, self-esteem, finances, etc... So I do the best I can to reach out and help others with my words. Why? Because I know that's what God put me on this earth to do.

That's my calling and purpose: to motivate and inspire. So I hope this book helped you in some way, as well as opened your eyes to a few things. And I hope you continue to support me, and watch me grow as an author/artist/designer/producer.

I won't let you down, I have a lot more books and art in the works.

Thank you for reading.

~ Shan

SHANNON BRANCH

www.ingramcontent.com/pod-product-compliance
Lightning Source LLC
Chambersburg PA
CBHW050545280326
41933CB00011B/1721